Grade 2

Spelling
PRACTICE BOOK
Annotated Teacher's Edition

Macmillan
McGraw-Hill

B

The *McGraw·Hill* Companies

Macmillan McGraw-Hill

Published by Macmillan/McGraw-Hill, of McGraw-Hill Education, a division of The McGraw-Hill Companies, Inc.,
Two Penn Plaza, New York, New York 10121.

Printed in the United States of America

4 5 6 7 8 9 10 021 09 08 07

Contents

Unit I • Relationships

School Days
David's New Friends
Short *a*

Practice 1
Word Sort 2
Word Meaning 3
Proofreading 4

Making Friends
Mr. Putter & Tabby Pour
the Tea
Short *o*

Practice 5
Word Sort 6
Word Meaning 7
Proofreading 8

Firefighters at Work
Time For Kids:
"Fighting the Fire"
Short *a*

Practice 9
Word Sort 10
Word Meaning 11
Proofreading 12

Being Yourself
Meet Rosina
Short *i*

Practice 13
Word Sort 14
Word Meaning 15
Proofreading 16

Coming to America
My Name Is Yoon
Short *o*

Practice 17
Word Sort 18
Word Meaning 19
Proofreading 20

Unit 2 • Growth and Change

Plants Alive!	Practice	21
The Tiny Seed	Word Sort	22
Short _u_	Word Meaning	23
	Proofreading	24
Animal Rescue	Practice	25
A Harbor Seal Pup	Word Sort	26
Grows Up	Word Meaning	27
Consonant Blends: Initial	Proofreading	28
and Final _sl, dr, sk, sp, st_		
A Hospital Visit	Practice	29
Time For Kids:	Word Sort	30
"A Trip to the	Word Meaning	31
Emergency Room"	Proofreading	32
Long _a_		
	Practice	33
How Animals Grow	Word Sort	34
Farfallina and Marcel	Word Meaning	35
Long _i_	Proofreading	36
Staying Fit	Practice	37
There's Nothing Like	Word Sort	38
Baseball	Word Meaning	39
Long _o_	Proofreading	40

Unit 3 • Better Together

Telling Stories
Head, Body, Legs:
A Story From Liberia
Long *e*

Practice 41
Word Sort 42
Word Meaning 43
Proofreading 44

Safety First
Officer Buckle and Gloria
Long *u*

Practice 45
Word Sort 46
Word Meaning 47
Proofreading 48

Creatures Old and Older
Time For Kids:
"Meet the Super Croc"
Consonant Digraphs
ch, sh, th, wh

Practice 49
Word Sort 50
Word Meaning 51
Proofreading 52

Curtain Up!
The Alvin Ailey Kids:
Dancing As a Team
Medial, Final Consonant
Digraphs *ch, tch, sh, th*

Practice 53
Word Sort 54
Word Meaning 55
Proofreading 56

On the Farm
Click, Clack, Moo:
Cows That Type
Initial Triple-Consonant
Blends *scr, spr, str*

Practice 57
Word Sort 58
Word Meaning 59
Proofreading 60

Unit 4 • Land, Sea, Sky

Animal Needs
Splish! Splash!
Animal Baths
r-Controlled
Vowels *ar, or*

Practice 61
Word Sort. 62
Word Meaning 63
Proofreading 64

Animal Survival
Goose's Story
r-Controlled
Vowels *er, ir, ur*

Practice 65
Word Sort. 66
Word Meaning 67
Proofreading 68

A Way to Help
Planet Earth
Time For Kids:
"A Way to Help
Planet Earth"
Variant Vowel *oo, ou*

Practice 69
Word Sort. 70
Word Meaning 71
Proofreading 72

Wild Weather
Super Storm
Variant Vowels *oo, ui, ew*

Practice 73
Word Sort. 74
Word Meaning 75
Proofreading 76

Habitats and Homes
Nutik, the Wolf Pup
Variant Vowels *au, aw*

Practice 77
Word Sort. 78
Word Meaning 79
Proofreading 80

Unit 5 • Discoveries

Life In the Desert
Dig, Wait, Listen:
A Desert Toad's Tale
Diphthong *ow, ou*

Practice 81
Word Sort 82
Word Meaning 83
Proofreading 84

Play Time!
Pushing Up the Sky
Diphthong *oi, oy*

Practice 85
Word Sort 86
Word Meaning 87
Proofreading 88

Exploration
Time For Kids:
"Columbus Explores
New Lands"
Schwa *a*

Practice 89
Word Sort 90
Word Meaning 91
Proofreading 92

In the Garden
The Ugly Vegetables
Consonants
gn, kn, wr, mb

Practice 93
Word Sort 94
Word Meaning 95
Proofreading 96

Our Moon
The Moon
Hard and Soft
Consonants *c, g*

Practice 97
Word Sort 98
Word Meaning 99
Proofreading 100

Unit 6 • Expressions

Count on a Celebration
Mice and Beans
Endings *-dge, -ge, -lge,*
-nge, -rge
Practice 101
Word Sort 102
Word Meaning 103
Proofreading 104

Creating Stories
Stirring Up Memories
r-**Controlled Vowels**
ar, are, air
Practice 105
Word Sort 106
Word Meaning 107
Proofreading 108

Worlds of Art
Time For Kids:
"Music of the Stone Age"
r-**Controlled Vowels**
er, eer, ere, ear
Practice 109
Word Sort 110
Word Meaning 111
Proofreading 112

Inventions Then
and Now
African-American
Inventors
r-**Controlled Vowels**
or, ore, oar
Practice 113
Word Sort 114
Word Meaning 115
Proofreading 116

Other People,
Other Places
Babu's Song
r-**Controlled Vowels**
ire, ure
Practice 117
Word Sort 118
Word Meaning 119
Proofreading 120

Name _____

Using the Word Study Steps

1. LOOK at the word.

2. SAY the word aloud.

3. STUDY the letters in the word.

4. WRITE the word.

5. CHECK the word.
   Did you spell the word right?
   If not, go back to step 1.

Spelling Words	
has	sat
wag	had
bad	fix
six	him
will	if

Puzzle

Solve the puzzle. Circle the six hidden spelling words.

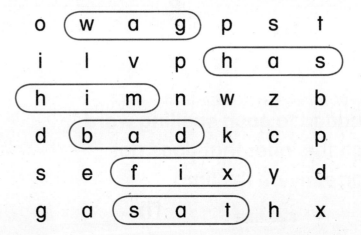

At Home: Review the Word Study Steps with your child as you both go over this week's spelling words.

David's New Friends • **Book 2.1/Unit 1**   1

Name_____

| has | six | him | sat | bad |
| wag | if | will | had | fix |

Word Sort

Look at the spelling words in the box. Write the spelling words that have the short *a* sound.

1. _____has_____ 2. _____sat_____ 3. _____bad_____

4. _____wag_____ 5. _____had_____

Write the spelling words that have the short *i* sound.

6. _____six_____ 7. _____him_____ 8. _____if_____

9. _____will_____ 10. _____fix_____

Misfit Letter

An extra letter has been added to each spelling word below. Draw a line through the letter that does not belong. Write the word correctly on the line.

11. hai̸s _____has_____   12. fixe̸ _____fix_____

13. say̸t _____sat_____   14. hy̸im _____him_____

15. wh̸ill _____will_____   16. iff̸ _____if_____

17. wage̸ _____wag_____   18. bai̸d _____bad_____

19. sixe̸ _____six_____   20. hay̸d _____had_____

Name_____

| has | six | him | sat | bad |
| wag | if | will | had | fix |

Match-Ups

Draw a line from each spelling word to its meaning.

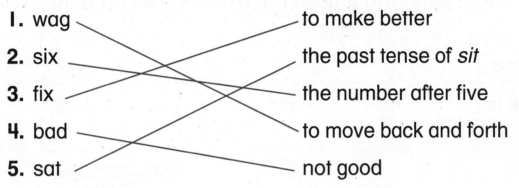

1. wag   to make better

2. six   the past tense of *sit*

3. fix   the number after five

4. bad   to move back and forth

5. sat   not good

Sentences to Complete

Write a spelling word on each line to complete the sentence.

6. I hope you ___**will**___ come to see my class tomorrow.

7. Can I help ___**him**___ with the test?

8. We ___**had**___ a new teacher last week.

9. Now Ted ___**has**___ a book on his desk.

10. What happens ___**if**___ my bus is late?

**There are six spelling mistakes in the paragraph below.
Circle the misspelled words. Write the words correctly
on the lines below.**

I (haid) a very good day at school. I got to help (fikx) the
fish tank. Then Mr. Dan and I (sayt) down. I told (hime) all
about a book I had read. He asked (iff) he could borrow it.
I said, "Yes, I (wil) bring it in so the whole class can read
it."

1. _____had_____   2. _____fix_____   3. _____sat_____
4. _____him_____   5. _____if_____   6. _____will_____

Writing

**Write about your day at school. Use three spelling words
from your list.**

_____

_____

_____

_____

Name_____

Using the Word Study Steps

1. LOOK at the word.

2. SAY the word aloud.

3. STUDY the letters in the word.

4. WRITE the word.

5. CHECK the word.
   Did you spell the word correctly?
   If not, go back to Step 1.

Spelling Words	
went	not
tell	tug
pet	hut
job	tub
fog	bun

Find and Circle

Circle the 10 hidden spelling words. The words are across, down, and on a slant.

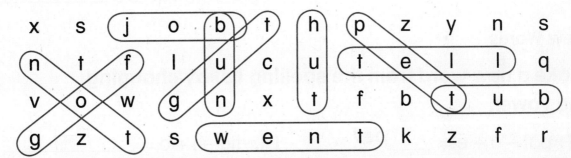

```
x   s   j   o   b   t   h   p   z   y   n   s
n   t   f   l   u   c   u   t   e   l   l   q
v   o   w   g   n   x   t   f   b   t   u   b
g   z   t   s   w   e   n   t   k   z   f   r
```

 At Home: Review the Word Study Steps with your child as you both go over this week's spelling words.

Mr. Putter & Tabby Pour the Tea
Book 2.1/Unit 1

 5

Name_____

went	tub	not	tug	fog
pet	tell	hut	job	bun

Word Sort

Look at the spelling words in the box. Match each word to a vowel sound. Write the words on the lines.

Short *e*	Short *o*	Short *u*
1. went	4. not	7. tub
2. pet	5. fog	8. tug
3. tell	6. job	9. hut
		10. bun

New Words

Make a new word from the spelling list by changing the vowel.

11. pat – a + e = __pet__   14. fig – i + o = __fog__

12. bin – i + u = __bun__   15. hat – a + u = __hut__

13. jab – a + o = __job__

Name_____

went	tub	not	tug	fog
pet	tell	hut	job	bun

Write a spelling word to complete each sentence.

1. Tom lets me _____**pet**_____ his dog.

2. I can _____**tell**_____ that Jen likes me.

3. Gus and I _____**went**_____ to the park.

4. It is _____**not**_____ nice to be mean.

5. I bathe my puppy in the _____**tub**_____.

6. Mike and Dan made a _____**hut**_____ to play in.

7. I did a good _____**job**_____ helping my friend.

8. At dinner Dad gave me a hamburger on a _____**bun**_____.

9. My dog likes to _____**tug**_____ on his leash.

10. The _____**fog**_____ makes it hard to see.

Name

There are six spelling mistakes in the letter below. Circle the misspelled words. Write the words correctly on the lines.

Dear Ben,

    I want to (tel) you about Sam. He is my new (peet) rabbit. I (weint) to the store and got him a cage and some food. He is (nat) very big yet. I gave him his first bath in the (tuab.) Taking care of him is a big (jaub.) Please come see him soon!

                    Your friend,

                    Matt

1. ___tell___ 2. ___pet___ 3. ___went___

4. ___not___ 5. ___tub___ 6. ___job___

Writing

Write a letter to a friend. Use three spelling words from the list.

_____

_____

_____

_____

Name_____

Using the Word Study Steps

1. LOOK at the word.

2. SAY the word aloud.

3. STUDY the letters in the word.

4. WRITE the word.

5. CHECK the word.
   Did you spell the word right?
   If not, go back to step 1.

Spelling Words	
bag	mad
cap	back
ham	cape
bake	made
ate	rake

Sounds the Same

Write a spelling word that rhymes with the words in each group.

1. dad   sad   _____mad_____

2. rate   date   _____ate_____

3. lake   make   _bake, rake_

4. map   lap   _____cap_____

5. nag   rag   _____bag_____

6. ram   jam   _____ham_____

© Macmillan/McGraw-Hill

 At Home: Review the Word Study Steps with your child as you both go over this week's spelling words.

Name_____

| cape | bake | mad | bag | rake |
| ate | back | cap | ham | made |

Word Sort

Look at the spelling words in the box. Write the spelling words that have the short *a* sound.

1. ____mad____ 2. ____bag____ 3. ____back____

4. ____cap____ 5. ____ham____

Write the spelling words that have the long *a* sound.

6. ____cape____ 7. ____bake____ 8. ____rake____

9. ____ate____ 10. ____made____

Word Find

Find and circle five spelling words in the puzzle.

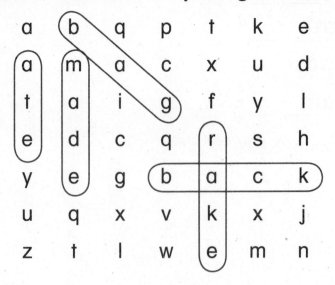

| cape | bake | mad | bag | rake |
| ate | back | cap | ham | made |

Questions

Write a spelling word to answer each question.

1. What can you use to make a pile of leaves? _____**rake**_____

2. What can taste good on a sandwich? _____**ham**_____

3. What can you put on your head? _____**cap**_____

4. What can you put your lunch in? _____**bag**_____

5. What word means not happy? _____**mad**_____

Sentences to Complete

Write a spelling word to complete each sentence.

6. I _____**ate**_____ an apple for lunch.

7. Dad _____**made**_____ a fire at camp.

8. We drove _____**back**_____ home after the show.

9. Kate wore a black _____**cape**_____ on her back.

10. I can _____**bake**_____ the bread in the oven.

Name_____

There is one spelling mistake in each sentence.
Circle the misspelled words. Write the correct words on
the lines below.

1. Dad and I got a (baig.)

2. We went (backe) to camp with lots of sticks.

3. Dad made a fire, and we (ayt) fish for dinner.

4. I was (maed) when it started to rain.

5. We (mayd) sure the fire was out.

1. ____bag____   2. ____back____   3. ____ate____

4. ____mad____   5. ____made____

Writing

Write about fire safety. Use three
spelling words from your list.

_____

_____

_____

_____

_____

Name_____

Using the Word Study Steps

1. LOOK at the word.

2. SAY the word aloud.

3. STUDY the letters in the word.

4. WRITE the word.

5. CHECK the word.
   Did you spell the word right?
   If not, go back to step 1.

Spelling Words	
did	rip
fin	mix
pick	five
nine	side
pipe	hike

X the Words

Put an X on the words with the long *i* sound.

rip	p**X**e	pick
h**X**e	fin	mix
si**X**e	did	n**X**e
fi**X**e	lit	wick
fit	lick	sip
fix	bit	win

 At Home: Review the Word Study Steps with your child as you both go over this week's spelling words.

Meet Rosina • Book 2.1/Unit 1   **13**

hike	did	rip	pipe	side
fin	mix	nine	five	pick

Word Sort

Look at the spelling words in the box. Write the spelling words that have the short *i* sound.

1. did   2. rip   3. fin

4. mix   5. pick

Write the spelling words that have the long *i* sound.

6. hike   7. pipe   8. side

9. nine   10. five

Sounds the Same

Write the spelling word that rhymes with each word below.

11. bike   hike

12. bin   fin

13. kid   did

14. ripe   pipe

15. fine   nine

16. dive   five

17. stick   pick

18. ride   side

19. fix   mix

20. dip   rip

© Macmillan/McGraw-Hill

Name_____

hike   did   rip   pipe   side

fin   mix   nine   five   pick

Match-Ups

Draw a line from each spelling word to its meaning.

1. rip   to walk in the woods

2. hike   part of a fish

3. pipe   to tear

4. mix   a metal tube

5. fin   to stir

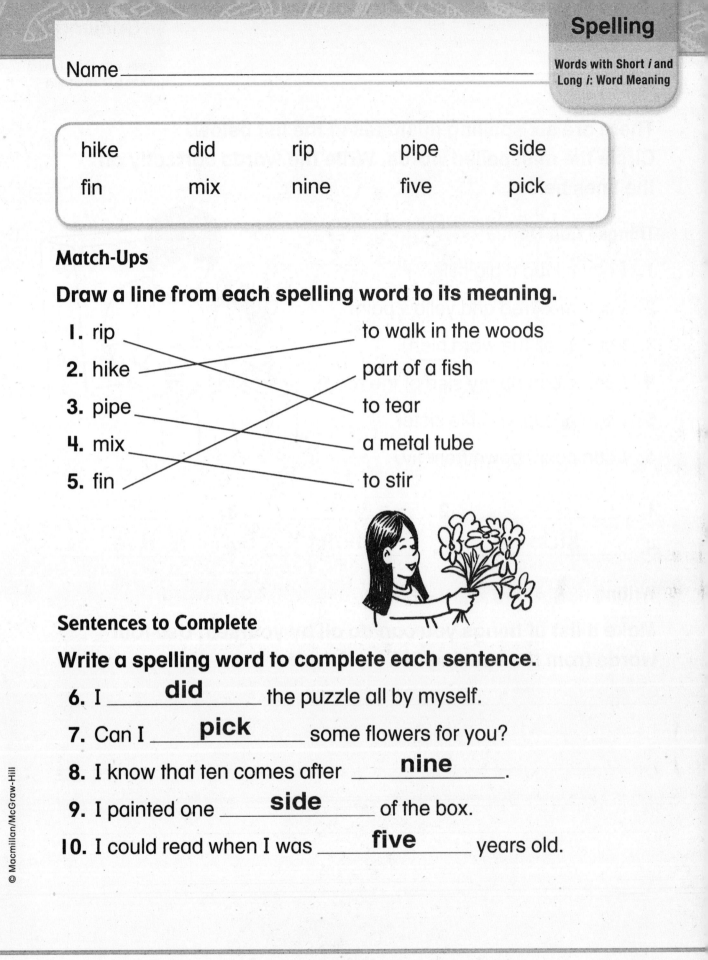

Sentences to Complete

Write a spelling word to complete each sentence.

6. I _____ **did** _____ the puzzle all by myself.

7. Can I _____ **pick** _____ some flowers for you?

8. I know that ten comes after _____ **nine** _____.

9. I painted one _____ **side** _____ of the box.

10. I could read when I was _____ **five** _____ years old.

Name_____

There are six spelling mistakes in the list below.
Circle the misspelled words. Write the words correctly on
the lines below.

Things I Can Do

1. I can (hik) up a big hill.

2. I can (mixx) red and yellow paint.

3. I can spell the word (nien.)

4. I can clean up my (sied) of the room.

5. I can (pik) up my little sister.

6. I can count down from (fiv.)

1. ____hike____ 2. ____mix____ 3. ____nine____

4. ____side____ 5. ____pick____ 6. ____five____

Writing

Make a list of things you can do all by yourself. Use four
words from the spelling list.

_____

_____

_____

© Macmillan/McGraw-Hill

Name_____

Using the Word Study Steps

1. LOOK at the word.

2. SAY the word aloud.

3. STUDY the letters in the word.

4. WRITE the word.

5. CHECK the word.
   Did you spell the word right?
   If not, go back to step 1.

Spelling Words	
dog	hope
fox	rope
lock	pot
rose	box
poke	cone

Puzzle

Solve the puzzle. Circle the five hidden spelling words.

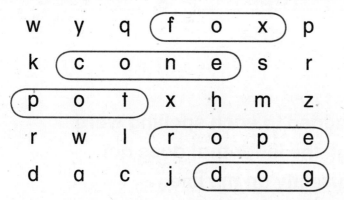

```
w   y   q   f   o   x   p
k   c   o   n   e   s   r
p   o   t   x   h   m   z
r   w   l   r   o   p   e
d   a   c   j   d   o   g
```

 At Home: Review the Word Study Steps with your child as
you both go over this week's spelling words.

My Name Is Yoon • **Book 2.1/Unit 1** 17

Name_____

| dog | lock | poke | rope | box |
| fox | rose | hope | pot | cone |

Word Sort

Look at the spelling words in the box. Write the spelling words that have the short *o* sound.

1. dog   2. lock   3. box

4. fox   5. pot

Write the spelling words that have the long *o* sound.

6. poke   7. rope   8. rose

9. hope   10. cone

Misfit Letter

An extra letter has been added to each spelling word below. Draw a line through the letter that does not belong. Write the word correctly on the line.

11. boxx __box__   12. roepe __rope__

13. dogg __dog__   14. coine __cone__

15. hopie __hope__   16. pooke __poke__

17. faox __fox__   18. locke __lock__

19. pout __pot__   20. roase __rose__

Name_____

dog	lock	poke	rope	box
fox	rose	hope	pot	cone

Make a Connection

Write a spelling word to complete each pair of sentences.

1. A cat purrs.

   A _____ **dog** _____ barks.

2. The skunk smelled bad.

   The _____ **rose** _____ smelled nice.

3. We made eggs in the pan.

   We made soup in the _____ **pot** _____.

4. The bear was black.

   The _____ **fox** _____ was red.

5. The bag was made of paper.

   The _____ **box** _____ was made of wood.

6. The string was easy to cut.

   The _____ **rope** _____ was hard to cut.

Sentences to Complete

Write a spelling word to complete each sentence.

7. Put the key in the _____ **lock** _____.

8. Mom put ice cream in the _____ **cone** _____.

9. I _____ **hope** _____ you can come to my party.

10. Do not _____ **poke** _____ me with the stick.

Name_____

There are five spelling mistakes in the paragraph below. Circle the misspelled words. Write the words correctly on the lines below.

There is a new girl in my class. I (hoape) we can be friends. I will show her where to put her lunch (boxe). I will tell her about my (doig). I can teach her how to play jump (roepe) at recess. Then we can have an ice cream (coyne) after school.

1. _____ hope _____   2. _____ box _____   3. _____ dog _____

4. _____ rope _____   5. _____ cone _____

Writing

Write about how you would become friends with a new boy or girl who came to your school. Use five words from the spelling list.

_____

_____

_____

_____

Name_____

Using the Word Study Steps

1. LOOK at the word.

2. SAY the word aloud.

3. STUDY the letters in the word.

4. WRITE the word.

5. CHECK the word.
   Did you spell the word right?
   If not, go back to step 1.

Spelling Words

sun	bud
duck	bump
cup	cube
dude	fume
rule	rude

Circle the Word

Circle the words with the long *u* sound.

duck	bump	cup	(cube)	(rude)
sun	(fume)	(dude)	(rule)	bud

 At Home: Review the Word Study Steps with your child as
you both go over this week's spelling words.

The Tiny Seed • Book 2.1/Unit 2   21

Name_____

| bud | rude | fume | sun | cup |
| dude | rule | duck | bump | cube |

Word Sort

Look at the spelling words in the box. Write each spelling word in the correct column.

Short *u* Words

1. bud
2. sun
3. cup
4. duck
5. bump

Long *u* Words

6. rude
7. fume
8. dude
9. rule
10. cube

Rhyme Time

Write the spelling word that rhymes with each of these words.

11. bun ___ sun
12. lump ___ bump
13. mud ___ bud
14. luck ___ duck
15. pup ___ cup

Name_____

has	sat	wag	had	bad
fix	six	him	will	if

Match-Ups

Draw a line from each spelling word to its meaning.

1. fume — something you drink from

2. cup — a smell

3. duck — a shape with six sides

4. cube — to hit

5. bump — a bird that swims

Sentences to Complete

Write a spelling word on each line to complete the sentence.

6. It is hot sitting in the _____**sun**_____.

7. It is not nice to be _____**rude**_____.

8. There is a pink _____**bud**_____ on the plant.

9. Please follow the class _____**rule**_____.

10. Gus is a cool _____**dude**_____.

Name_____

There are five spelling mistakes in the paragraph below. Circle the misspelled words. Write the words correctly on the lines below.

Dad and I planted seeds today. We put them where they would get lots of (suen). I gave each seed a (cuip) of water. I made a sign with a (ruel) The sign said: *Please do not (bummp) the plants.* I can't wait until we see the first (bude).

1. _____sun_____   2. _____cup_____   3. _____rule_____

4. _____bump_____   5. _____bud_____

Please do not bump the plants.

Writing

Write about planting or taking care of seeds. Use five spelling words from your list.

_____

_____

_____

_____

_____

Name_____

Using the Word Study Steps

1. LOOK at the word.

2. SAY the word aloud.

3. STUDY the letters in the word.

4. WRITE the word.

5. CHECK the word.
   Did you spell the word right?
   If not, go back to step 1.

Spelling Words	
slide	task
slips	still
dress	must
drop	crisp
skin	spell

Word Builder

Be a word builder. Write the missing consonant to finish each spelling word.

1. s __l__ ips

2. d __r__ ess

3. s __p__ ell

4. mus __t__

5. d __r__ op

6. s __k__ in

7. tas __k__

8. s __l__ ide

9. s __t__ ill

10. cris __p__

At Home: Review the Word Study Steps with your child as you both go over this week's spelling words.

A Harbor Seal Pup Grows Up

Book 2.1/Unit 2

© Macmillan/McGraw-Hill

Name_____

| drop | skin | task | spell | crisp |
| slide | must | still | dress | slips |

Word Sort

Find the spelling words that begin or end with each of the sounds below. Write the words in the correct box.

sl

1. _____slide_____
2. _____slips_____

dr

3. _____drop_____
4. _____dress_____

dr

5. _____skin_____
6. _____task_____

st

7. _____must_____
8. _____still_____

sp

9. _____spell_____
10. _____crisp_____

Pattern Smart

Write the spelling words that have the same pattern as *drum*.

11. _____drop_____ 12. _____dress_____

Write the spelling words that have the same pattern as *slap*.

13. _____slide_____ 14. _____slips_____

15. **Where do these letters appear? Circle the answer.**

(at the beginning)   at the end

© Macmillan/McGraw-Hill

Name_____

| dress | task | drop | skin | still |
| slips | must | crisp | spell | slide |

Not the Same

On the line beside each word, write the spelling word
that means the opposite.

1. pick up _____ **drop** _____

2. soggy _____ **crisp** _____

3. undress _____ **dress** _____

4. moving _____ **still** _____

Sentences to Complete

Write a spelling word on each line to complete the
sentence.

6. Can I go down the _____ **slide** _____?

7. I can _____ **spell** _____ a lot of words.

8. My _____ **skin** _____ is red from the sun.

9. Dad and Mom _____ **must** _____ pay their bills.

10. The _____ **task** _____ was to wash the windows.

**There are five spelling mistakes in the diary entry below.
Circle the misspelled words. Write the words correctly
on the lines below.**

May 10 Today I found a stray kitten. I knew I (musk)
take care of her. I took her inside. I think she was so
scared that she sat (stille.) I gave her a (dropp) of milk. She
liked it! She started to lick her fur. Her (scin) was red. I will
need to take her to the vet. Finding who owns her will not
be a easy (tassk.) But I know I will!

1. _____**must**_____   2. _____**still**_____   3. _____**drop**_____

4. _____**skin**_____   5. _____**task**_____

Writing

**Write about how you would help rescue
an animal. Use five spelling words from the list.**

_____

_____

_____

_____

Name_____

Using the Word Study Steps

1. LOOK at the word.

2. SAY the word aloud.

3. STUDY the letters in the word.

4. WRITE the word.

5. CHECK the word.
   Did you spell the word right?
   If not, go back to step 1.

Spelling Words	
main	jay
wait	pay
sail	stay
tail	hay
train	may

Find and Circle

Where are the spelling words?

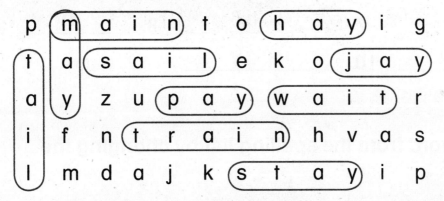

p m a i n t o h a y i g
t a s a i l e k o j a y
a y z u p a y w a i t r
i f n t r a i n h v a s
l m d a j k s t a y i p

At Home: Review the Word Study Steps with your child as you both go over this week's spelling words.

Name_____

| jay | may | wait | sail | train |
| hay | main | tail | pay | stay |

Write the Words

Write the spelling words that have the long *a* sound spelled *ai*.

1. wait   2. sail   3. train

4. main   5. tail

Write the spelling words that have the long *a* sound spelled *ay*.

6. jay   7. may   8. hay

9. pay   10. stay

New Words

Make a new word from the spelling list by changing the first letter.

11. way – w + j = jay

12. mail – m + t = tail

13. day – d + h = hay

14. gain – g + m = main

15. brain – b + t = train

Name_____

tail	stay	pay	main	wait
may	sail	hay	jay	train

Sentences to Complete

Write the spelling word on each line to complete the sentence.

1. I have to _____**pay**_____ a quarter for the milk.

2. My dog wags his _____**tail**_____ when he is happy.

3. Do you know how to _____**sail**_____ a boat?

4. Will you _____**wait**_____ for me to get there?

5. I _____**may**_____ not go to the game today.

6. What time does the _____**train**_____ come?

7. Grandma will _____**stay**_____ at our house.

8. Is that a blue _____**jay**_____ in the tree?

9. There were lots of shops on the _____**main**_____ street.

10. There is plenty of _____**hay**_____ in the barn.

Name_____

There are five spelling mistakes in the paragraph below. Circle the misspelled words. Write the words correctly on the lines below.

Today my mom fell and hurt her arm. My dad thought she (mae) need a cast. We all went to the hospital. We needed to see the (mayn) doctor. We had to (waet) our turn. Then my mom got an x-ray. She did need a cast. The doctor told her to (staiy) still. My dad left to (paye) the bill. At last, we all went home and signed Mom's new cast.

1. ____**may**____   2. ____**main**____   3. ____**wait**____

4. ____**stay**____   5. ____**pay**____

Writing

Write about how you would help someone who got hurt or who was sick. Use five spelling words from your list.

_____

_____

_____

_____

_____

Name_____

Using the Word Study Steps

1. LOOK at the word.

2. SAY the word aloud.

3. STUDY the letters in the word.

4. WRITE the word.

5. CHECK the word.
   Did you spell the word right?
   If not, go back to step 1.

Spelling Words	
light	high
sight	wild
mind	dry
cry	try
tie	lie

X the Words

Put an X on the words with the long *i* sound.

d~~ry~~	dip	pick	l~~ie~~	rip
sit	si~~g~~ht	mit	t~~ry~~	m~~i~~nd
w~~i~~ld	tip	hi~~g~~h	clip	t~~ie~~
hill	c~~ry~~	li~~g~~ht	tilt	will

 At Home: Review the Word Study Steps with your child as you both go over this week's spelling words.

Farfallina and Marcel
Book 2.1/Unit 2

33

Name _____

| light | lie | try | high | tie |
| wild | mind | sight | cry | dry |

Write the Words

Write the spelling words that have the long *i* sound spelled *i*.

1. _____wild_____   2. _____mind_____

Write the spelling words that have the long *i* sound spelled *ie*.

3. _____lie_____   4. _____tie_____

Write the spelling words that have the long *i* sound spelled *y*.

5. _____try_____   6. _____cry_____   7. _____dry_____

Write the spelling words that have the long *i* sound spelled *igh*.

8. _____light_____   9. _____high_____   10. _____sight_____

Misfit Letter

An extra letter has been added to each spelling word below. Draw a line through the letter that does not belong. Write the word correctly on the line.

11. highe _____high_____   12. miend _____mind_____

13. crye _____cry_____   14. tyie _____tie_____

15. wiled _____wild_____

Name_____

light	lie	try	high	tie
wild	mind	sight	cry	dry

Word Meaning

Find the opposite. Draw lines to connect the spelling words to words that mean the opposite.

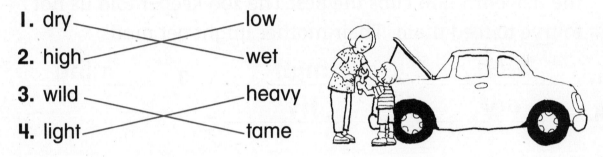

1. dry — low
2. high — wet
3. wild — heavy
4. light — tame

Sentences to Complete

Write a spelling word on each line to complete the sentence.

5. Can you _____ **tie** _____ your shoes?

6. I will _____ **try** _____ to help you fix the car.

7. You look sad when you _____ **cry** _____.

8. Your _____ **sight** _____ is what helps you see.

9. Do you _____ **mind** _____ if I sit next to you?

10. You should never tell a _____ **lie** _____.

Name _____

**There are five spelling mistakes in the report below.
Circle the misspelled words. Write the words correctly
on the lines below.**

Our class took a trip to the zoo. We saw tame animals
and (wield) animals. There was a baby kangaroo. He
could jump (highe). We did not (miend) getting splashed by
the baby seal pups. We sat in the sun to get (driy). We liked
the newborn lion cubs the best. The zoo keeper told us not
to (trye) to feed them. Their mother might get mad!

1. _____**wild**_____ 2. _____**high**_____ 3. _____**mind**_____

4. _____**dry**_____ 5. _____**try**_____

Writing

**Write a report about baby or adult animals. Use five
words from the spelling list.**

_____

_____

_____

_____

© Macmillan/McGraw-Hill

Name_____

Using the Word Study Steps

1. LOOK at the word.

2. SAY the word aloud.

3. STUDY the letters in the word.

4. WRITE the word.

5. CHECK the word.
   Did you spell the word right?
   If not, go back to step 1.

Spelling Words

grow	toast
mow	soap
crow	foam
toe	told
goes	most

Crossword Puzzle

Write the spelling word that best matches each clue. Put the spelling words in the boxes that start with the same number.

ACROSS

2. past tense of *tell*

3. almost all

7. to get bigger

8. what you wash with

DOWN

1. moves

3. to cut grass

4. to heat bread

5. a bird

6. soap bubbles

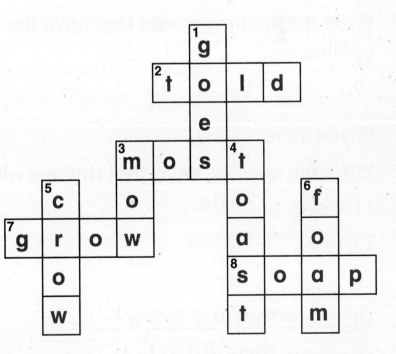

 At Home: Review the Word Study Steps with your child as you both go over this week's spelling words.

most	mow	goes	toast	foam
grow	told	crow	toe	soap

Write the Words

Write the spelling words that have the long _o_ sound spelled _o_.

1. _____told_____   2. _____most_____

Write the spelling words that have the long _o_ sound spelled _oa_.

3. _____toast_____   4. _____foam_____   5. _____soap_____

Write the spelling words that have the long _o_ sound spelled _ow_.

6. _____mow_____   7. _____grow_____   8. _____crow_____

Write the spelling words that have the long _o_ sound spelled _oe_.

9. _____toe_____   10. _____goes_____

Rhyme Time

Write the spelling word that rhymes with each of these words.

11. cold _____told_____

12. hoes _____goes_____

13. rope _____soap_____

14. doe _____toe/mow/crow_____

15. roast _____toast/most_____

Name_____

| toast | soap | mow | goes | crow |
| grow | toe | told | most | foam |

Sentences to Complete

Write a spelling word on each line to complete the sentence.

1. I _____**told**_____ my friend to wait for me after class.

2. What color are _____**most**_____ trees?

3. Dad will _____**mow**_____ the grass today.

4. Mom made eggs and _____**toast**_____.

5. There is a bar of _____**soap**_____ on the sink.

6. A _____**crow**_____ is a black bird.

7. Did you _____**grow**_____ an inch taller?

8. I stubbed my _____**toe**_____ on the step.

9. Joe _____**goes**_____ to work at nine.

10. The soap made bubbles and _____**foam**_____.

Name_____

**There are five spelling mistakes in the paragraph below.
Circle the misspelled words. Write the words correctly
on the lines below.**

When I (groe) up I want to play baseball like my brother.
He (gois) to practice every day. He (tolde) me that he works
hard to be a good player. He has never missed a game.
Once he even played with a broken (tow.) What he loves
(moast) about baseball is that it helps keep him in shape.

1. _____grow_____   2. _____goes_____   3. _____told_____

4. _____toe_____   5. _____most_____

Writing

**What sport or activity keeps
you in good shape? Write about it.
Use five spelling words from your list.**

_____

_____

_____

_____

Name_____

Using the Word Study Steps

1. LOOK at the word.

2. SAY the word aloud.

3. STUDY the letters in the word.

4. WRITE the word.

5. CHECK the word.
   Did you spell the word right?
   If not, go back to step 1.

Spelling Words	
eat	leaf
mean	queen
need	seek
baby	pony
he	we

Puzzle

Solve the puzzle. Circle the ten hidden spelling words.

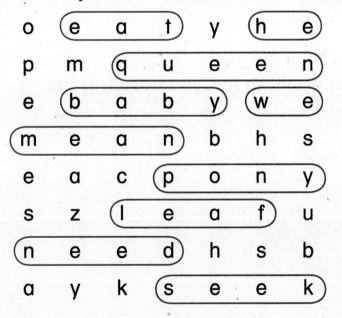

At Home: Review the Word Study Steps with your child as
you both go over this week's spelling words.

Head, Body, Legs: A Story
from Liberia • **Book 2.1/Unit 3**

41

Name

need	baby	we	queen	eat
leaf	he	mean	seek	pony

Word Sort

Fill in the blanks below with spelling words that match each spelling pattern.

e	*ee*	*ea*	*y*
1. we	3. need	6. eat	9. baby
2. he	4. queen	7. leaf	10. pony
	5. seek	8. mean	

New Words

Make a new word from the spelling list by changing the first letter.

11. seed – s + n __need__

12. be – b + w __we__

13. lean – l + m __mean__

14. me – m + h __he__

15. peek – p + s __seek__

Name_____

pony   he   seek   mean   need

leaf   eat   baby   we   queen

Match-Ups

Draw a line from each spelling word to its meaning.

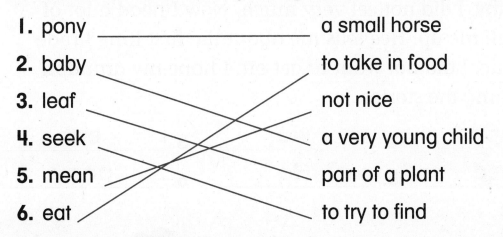

1. pony _____   a small horse

2. baby   to take in food

3. leaf   not nice

4. seek   a very young child

5. mean   part of a plant

6. eat   to try to find

Sentences to Complete

**Write a spelling word on each line to complete
the sentence.**

7. Can _____**we**_____ all go to the play with you?

8. The king and _____**queen**_____ wore crowns.

9. How will _____**he**_____ find his way home?

10. I _____**need**_____ to get some sleep.

Name _____

There are six spelling mistakes in the paragraph below. Circle the misspelled words. Write the words correctly on the lines below.

My grandpa likes to tell stories. He tells me about things I did when I was a little (babie) He remembers when (wey) went to the park together. He says that when I was a baby, I did not (eet) very much. Now I (nead) a lot of food to fill me up! (Hee) tells me about the first time I rode on a (ponie). I did not want to get off. I hope my grandpa keeps telling me stories.

1. _____ baby _____   2. _____ we _____   3. _____ eat _____

4. _____ need _____   5. _____ He _____   6. _____ pony _____

Writing

Write a family story. Use four words from the spelling list. Share and compare your story with a classmate's story.

_____

_____

_____

Name _____

Using the Word Study Steps

1. LOOK at the word.

2. SAY the word aloud.

3. STUDY the letters in the word.

4. WRITE the word.

5. CHECK the word.
   Did you spell the word right?
   If not, go back to step 1.

Spelling Words	
mule	June
bugle	music
fuse	duke
use	tune
flute	dune

X the Words

Put an X on the words with the long *u* sound.

hut	fu**X**e	bun	bu**X**le	button
tu**X**e	rug	du**X**e	u**X**e	us
bug	mu**X**ic	luck	du**X**e	m**X**le
flu**X**e	much	cup	Ju**X**e	sun

At Home: Review the Word Study Steps with your child as you both go over this week's spelling words.

Officer Buckle and Gloria
Book 2.1/Unit 3

45

© Macmillan/McGraw-Hill

Name_____

flute	tune	dune	use	June
mule	duke	bugle	music	fuse

Word Sort

Look at the spelling words in the box. Write the spelling words that have the long *u* sound spelled *u*.

1. _____bugle_____   2. _____music_____

Write the spelling words that have the long *u* sound spelled *u_e*.

3. _____flute_____   4. _____tune_____   5. _____dune_____

6. _____use_____   7. _____June_____   8. _____mule_____

9. _____duke_____   10. _____fuse_____

Puzzle

Solve the puzzle. Circle the five hidden spelling words.

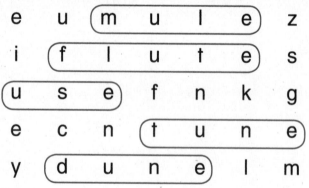

```
e   u  (m   u   l   e)  z
i  (f   l   u   t   e)  s
(u   s   e)  f   n   k   g
e   c   n  (t   u   n   e)
y  (d   u   n   e)  l   m
```

© Macmillan/McGraw-Hill

Name_____

flute   tune   dune   use   June

mule   duke   bugle   music   fuse

Match-Ups

Draw a line from each spelling word to its meaning.

1. June —————————— a sand hill

2. flute —————————— the month before July

3. dune —————————— a nobleman

4. mule —————————— an animal like a donkey

5. duke —————————— a wind instrument

Sentences to Complete

Write a spelling word on each line to complete the sentence.

6. I like _____**music**_____ class because I get to play the drums.

7. A _____**fuse**_____ blew so all the lights went out.

8. A _____**bugle**_____ is like a trumpet.

9. Can I _____**use**_____ your pen to write a note?

10. Dad hums a _____**tune**_____ when he rocks the baby.

There are five spelling mistakes in the list of rules below.
Circle the misspelled words. Write the words correctly
on the lines below.

Rules for Music Class

1. Do not (uise) instruments without asking the teacher.

2. (Tuune) your instrument before class begins.

3. Make sure no one will trip on your (buggle.)

4. Keep your (fluit) in the case unless you are playing it.

5. Put all of the (musec) books in a neat stack before you
   leave.

1. ____use____ 2. ____Tune____ 3. ____bugle____

4. ____flute____ 5. ____music____

Writing

Write about other school rules that
are important to follow. Use five
spelling words from your list.

_____

_____

_____

_____

Name_____

Using the Word Study Steps

1. LOOK at the word.

2. SAY the word aloud.

3. STUDY the letters in the word.

4. WRITE the word.

5. CHECK the word.
   Did you spell the word right?
   If not, go back to step 1.

Spelling Words

chest	chill
chase	shape
sheep	thing
think	white
while	wheat

Find and Circle

Where are the spelling words?

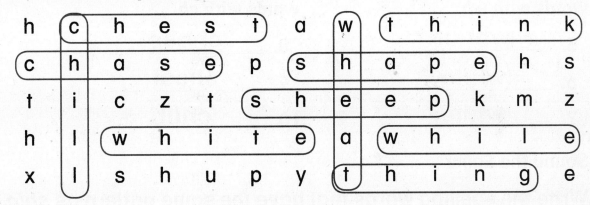

```
h  c  h  e  s  t  a  w  t  h  i  n  k
c  h  a  s  e  p  s  h  a  p  e  h  s
t  i  c  z  t  s  h  e  e  p  k  m  z
h  l  w  h  i  t  e  a  w  h  i  l  e
x  l  s  h  u  p  y  t  h  i  n  g  e
```

At Home: Review the Word Study Steps with your child as you both go over this week's spelling words.

Name_____

| chase | wheat | think | chest | shape |
| sheep | white | chill | thing | while |

Word Sort

Look at the spelling words in the box. Write the spelling words that follow the patterns below.

words with *th*

1. think
2. thing

words with *sh*

3. shape
4. sheep

words with *wh*

5. wheat
6. white
7. while

words with *ch*

8. chase
9. chest
10. chill

Sound the Same

Write the spelling words that have the same pattern as *ship*.

11. sheep
12. shape

Write the spelling words that have the same pattern as *cheap*.

13. chase
14. chest
15. chill

16. Circle the letters that spell the pattern in each word you wrote. Where do these letters appear? Circle the answer.

at the beginning   in the middle   at the end

© Macmillan/McGraw-Hill

Name

thing	sheep	chill	shape	wheat
chest	while	chase	white	think

Opposites

Draw a line to connect the words that mean the opposite.

1. chill   black
2. white   warm up
3. chase   let go

Sentences to Complete

Write a spelling word on each line to complete the sentence.

4. A circle is a round __**shape**__.

5. Wool comes from __**sheep**__.

6. I __**think**__ we should go home now.

7. Mom reads the map __**while**__ Dad drives.

8. Is there __**wheat**__ in the bread?

9. The toy __**chest**__ was filled with blocks.

10. What __**thing**__ is big, red, and shiny?

Name_____

**There are six spelling mistakes in the paragraph. Circle
the misspelled words. Write the words correctly on the
lines below.**

Julie and I were digging in the dirt. Julie found a (whiet)
rock. The (shaip) of the rock was round. She looked closely
at the rock (whyle) I kept on digging. Julie said, "I (thinke)
this might be a fossil. I see a (thinng) that looks like a
bone." Then a (chille) ran up my spine. Could this be the
fossil of a dinosaur?

1. ___**white**___   2. ___**shape**___   3. ___**while**___

4. ___**think**___   5. ___**thing**___   6. ___**chill**___

Writing

**Write about what it would be like to find the fossil of an
animal that lived millions of years ago. Use four spelling
words from your list.**

Answers will vary.

_____

_____

_____

_____

© Macmillan/McGraw-Hill

Name_____

Using the Word Study Steps

1. LOOK at the word.

2. SAY the word aloud.

3. STUDY the letters in the word.

4. WRITE the word.

5. CHECK the word.
   Did you spell the word right?
   If not, go back to step 1.

Spelling Words

each	which
teaching	path
teeth	fishing
wishbone	watch
matching	dish

X the Word

**Look at the end part of the spelling words in each row.
Put an X on the word that does not belong.**

1. wa~~t~~ch   matching   fishing

2. each   di~~s~~h   which

3. fishing   wish~~b~~one   matching

4. path   teeth   ea~~c~~h

5. teaching   matching   wa~~t~~ch

 At Home: Review the Word Study Steps with your child as you both go over this week's spelling words.

The Alvin Ailey Kids: Dancing As a Team • **Book 2.1/Unit 3** 53

Name_____

which	teaching	each	dish	matching
path	wishbone	teeth	fishing	watch

Pattern Power

Write the spelling words for each of these patterns.

th

1. _____path_____

2. _____teeth_____

sh

3. _____dish_____

4. _____wishbone_____

5. _____fishing_____

ch

6. _____which_____

7. _____teaching_____

8. _____each_____

tch

9. _____matching_____

10. _____watch_____

Rhyme Time

Write the spelling word that rhymes with each of these words.

11. peach _____each_____

12. bath _____path_____

13. fish _____dish_____

14. rich _____which_____

15. reaching _____teaching_____

Name _____

teeth	watch	dish	matching	each
which	teaching	path	wishbone	fishing

Sentences to Complete

Write a spelling word on each line to complete the sentence.

1. Trish put her sandwich on a ____**dish**____.

2. Hold the ____**wishbone**____ and make a wish.

3. Brush your ____**teeth**____ three times a day.

4. We rode our bikes on the dirt ____**path**____.

5. I don't know ____**which**____ street to take.

6. What time does your ____**watch**____ say?

7. Mitch got ____**each**____ one of us a gift.

Word Building

Add -ing to each word. Write the spelling word.

8. teach + ing = ____**teaching**____

9. fish + ing = ____**fishing**____

10. match + ing = ____**matching**____

**There are six spelling mistakes in the invitation below.
Circle the misspelled words. Write the words correctly on
the lines below.**

Dear Parents,

Please come to our class play. Mrs. Jones is (teashing) us
some new songs. (Eatch) one of us will have a special part.
We are going to wear (matshing) costumes and hats. We
hope you will come and (wach) us!

The play is in the gym. Follow the red (pacth) to find
your seat. The shows are Friday, Saturday, and Sunday.
(Whitch) show will you come to see?

1. ___teaching___ 2. ___Each___ 3. ___matching___

4. ___watch___ 5. ___path___ 6. ___Which___

Writing

**Invite someone to come
watch you sing, dance,
or perform something
special. Use four spelling
words from your list.**

_____

_____

_____

Name_____

Using the Word Study Steps

1. LOOK at the word.

2. SAY the word aloud.

3. STUDY the letters in the word.

4. WRITE the word.

5. CHECK the word.
   Did you spell the word right?
   If not, go back to step 1.

Spelling Words

screen	strict
scream	sprain
scrape	spring
stripe	spruce
struck	strap

Find and Circle

Where are the spelling words?

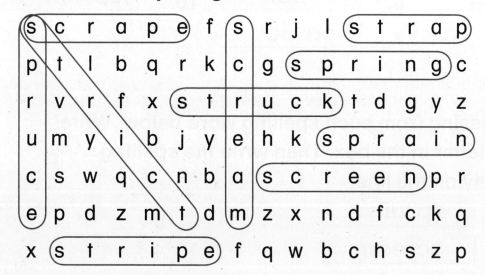

 At Home: Review the Word Study Steps with your child as you both go over this week's spelling words.

Name_____

strap	spruce	strict	struck	scream
scrape	spring	sprain	stripe	screen

Word Sort

Find the spelling words that begin with each of the letters below. Write the words on the lines.

scr

1. scream
2. scrape
3. screen

str

4. strap
5. strict
6. struck
7. stripe

spr

8. spruce
9. spring
10. sprain

Missing Letter

A letter is missing from each spelling word below. Write the missing letter in the box. Then write the spelling word correctly on the line.

11. spain ☐r sprain
12. sream ☐c scream
13. srict ☐t strict
14. spuce ☐r spruce
15. sripe ☐t stripe

© Macmillan/McGraw-Hill

Name _____

spring	strap	spruce	strict	screen
scream	scrape	stripe	struck	sprain

Match-Ups

Draw a line from each spelling word to its meaning.

1. scrape   to yell

2. scream   the season after winter

3. sprain   a kind of tree

4. spruce   a leather or cloth band

5. strap   to rub

6. spring   to twist a muscle

Sentences to Complete

Write a spelling word on each line to complete the sentence.

7. The ____**screen**____ on the window keeps the bugs out.

8. Dan had a red ____**stripe**____ on his soccer uniform.

9. Last time I was up to bat I ____**struck**____ out.

10. Our principal is very ____**strict**____ about school rules.

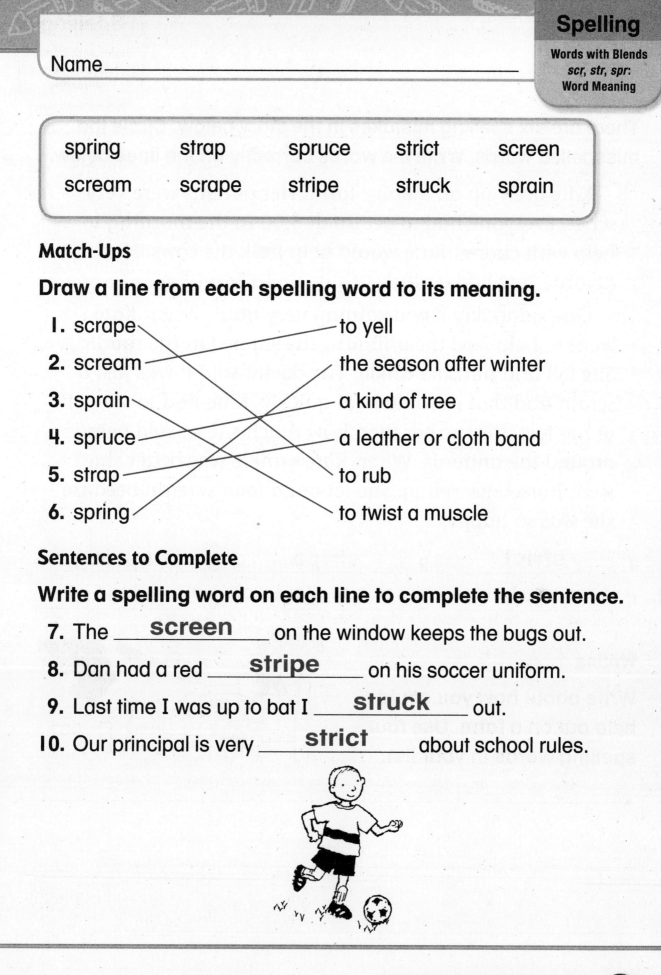

Name_____

There are six spelling mistakes in the story below. Circle the misspelled words. Write the words correctly on the lines below.

Kate grew up on a dairy farm. Her parents were very (scrict.) Everyone had to get up at 5:00 in the morning to help with chores. Kate would help milk the cows. Her favorite cow had a black (strippe) on its front leg.

One (sping) day it was raining very hard. When Kate went to help feed the animals, she slipped in the mud. She fell and hurt her ankle. The doctor said it was just a (scrain) and that it would heal quickly. Kate had to stay off of her feet. It (struc) her then how much she missed being around the animals. When Kate's ankle was better she went horseback riding. She let out a loud (skream) because she was so happy.

1. ____strict____   2. ____stripe____   3. ____spring____
4. ____sprain____   5. ____struck____   6. ____scream____

Writing

Write about how you could help out on a farm. Use four spelling words in your list.

© Macmillan/McGraw-Hill

_____

_____

_____

_____

Name_____

Using the Word Study Steps

1. LOOK at the word.

2. SAY the word aloud.

3. STUDY the letters in the word.

4. WRITE the word.

5. CHECK the word.
   Did you spell the word right?
   If not, go back to step 1.

Spelling Words	
part	sort
start	storm
park	short
farm	for
dark	horse

Find and Circle

Solve the puzzle. Circle the ten hidden spelling words.

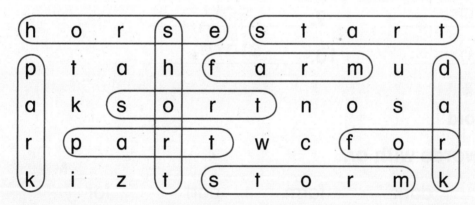

 At Home: Review the Word Study Steps with your child as you both go over this week's spelling words.

Splish! Splash! Animal Baths
Book 2.2/Unit 4
 61

© Macmillan/McGraw-Hill

Name_____

| horse | for | part | start | short |
| farm | park | sort | dark | storm |

Word Sort

Look at the spelling words in the box. Match each word to a spelling pattern.

ar

1. part
2. start
3. farm
4. park
5. dark

or

6. horse
7. for
8. short
9. sort
10. storm

Circle the Word

Circle the words with *or*.

(short)   dark   farm   part   (for)

start   (sort)   (horse)   (storm)   park

Name _____

dark	farm	storm	for	part
horse	short	start	park	sort

Opposites

Write the spelling word that means the opposite of each word below.

1. stop _____ **start**

2. light _____ **dark**

3. long _____ **short**

Sentences to Complete

Write a spelling word on the line to complete the sentence.

4. Sam has the biggest ___**part**___ in the play.

5. Cows and pigs live on a ___**farm**___.

6. I have a gift ___**for**___ my best friend.

7. Do you know how to ride a ___**horse**___?

8. Sue has to ___**sort**___ the socks by color.

9. We heard thunder during the ___**storm**___.

10. There are swings and a slide at the ___**park**___.

© Macmillan/McGraw-Hill

Name_____

There are six spelling mistakes in the paragraph below. Circle the misspelled words. Write the words correctly on the lines below.

My dog can run in the (perk). During a (starm) my dog hides under the couch. After (dirk) my dog sleeps in bed with me. A (herse) is too big to sleep in a bed. It lives in a stable on a (faerm). A horse likes to run (fer) miles. It eats a lot of food. I think a dog is easier to take care of than a horse.

1. ____park____   2. ____storm____   3. ____dark____

4. ____horse____   5. ____farm____   6. ____for____

Writing

Write about the needs of two different animals. Use four words from your spelling list.

_____

_____

_____

_____

_____

Name_____

Using the Word Study Steps

1. LOOK at the word.

2. SAY the word aloud.

3. STUDY the letters in the word.

4. WRITE the word.

5. CHECK the word.
   Did you spell the word right?
   If not, go back to step 1.

Spelling Words	
clerk	term
herd	skirt
sir	stir
churn	burst
hurt	turn

Word Builder

Be a word builder. Write the missing vowel to finish each spelling word.

1. c l __e__ r k

2. t __u__ r n

3. h __u__ r t

4. s __i__ r

5. t __e__ r m

6. h __e__ r d

7. c h __u__ r n

8. b __u__ r s t

9. s t __i__ r

10. s k __i__ r t

At Home: Review the Word Study Steps with your child as you both go over this week's spelling words.

Name_____

| term | hurt | sir | herd | stir |
| skirt | clerk | churn | burst | turn |

Word Sort

Look at the spelling words in the box. Match each word with a spelling pattern.

er 1. ____term____   2. ____herd____   3. ____clerk____

ir 4. ____sir____   5. ____stir____   6. ____skirt____

ur 7. ____hurt____   8. ____churn____   9. ____burst____

10. ____turn____

Misfit Letter

An extra letter has been added to each spelling word below. Draw a line through the letter that does not belong. Write the word correctly on the line.

11. sti~~e~~r ____stir____

12. h~~l~~erd ____herd____

13. cl~~l~~erk ____clerk____

14. hu~~e~~rt ____hurt____

15. ch~~e~~urn ____churn____

Name_____

churn	burst	clerk	skirt	term
sir	hurt	turn	stir	herd

Sentences to Complete

Write a spelling word on each line to complete the sentence.

1. The ____**clerk**____ in the store waited on us.

2. Trish wore a ____**skirt**____ and a sweater to the dance.

3. The first school ____**term**____ is over in November.

4. You can call the man ____**sir**____ to be polite.

5. Please take your ____**turn**____ in the game.

Word Meaning

Say it another way. Draw a line from each spelling word to the word or words that mean almost the same.

6. burst   mix

7. stir   pop

8. herd   stir milk

9. hurt   wounded

10. churn   large group

Spelling

Words with *r*-Controlled
Vowels: *er, ir, ur*:
Proofreading

Name _____

There are five spelling mistakes in the paragraph below. Circle the misspelled words. Write the words correctly on the lines below.

Animals have many different needs. Jason knows this from helping on his father's ranch. It is Jason's (tirn) to help with the cattle. There is a large (hurd.) They all need to stay together. Jason also needs to make sure that none of the cattle gets (hert.) Jason needs to (stur) a special medicine into the food of one cow that is sick. This is a big job. It takes a (berst) of energy for Jason to take care of the whole herd.

1. ___turn___   2. ___herd___   3. ___hurt___

4. ___stir___   5. ___burst___

Writing

Write a paragraph about the needs of one of your favorite animals. Use five words from your spelling list.

_____

_____

_____

_____

Name_____

Using the Word Study Steps

1. LOOK at the word.

2. SAY the word aloud.

3. STUDY the letters in the word.

4. WRITE the word.

5. CHECK the word.
   Did you spell the word right?
   If not, go back to step 1.

Spelling Words	
shook	stood
hook	brook
crook	foot
soot	could
should	would

Find and Circle

Where are the spelling words?

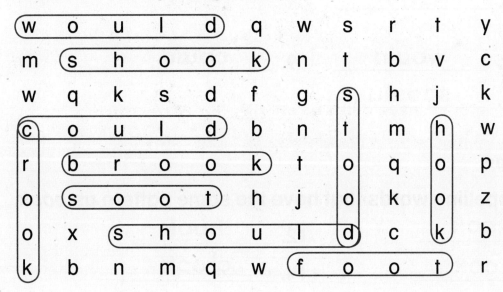

At Home: Review the Word Study Steps with your child as you both go over this week's spelling words.

Helping Planet Earth
Book 2.2/Unit 4
69

Name_____

would	shook	should	hook	could
soot	brook	foot	crook	stood

Word Sort

Look at the spelling words in the box. Match the spelling word with the spelling pattern and write the word.

oot   1. __soot__   2. __foot__

ook   3. __shook__   4. __hook__
        5. __brook__   6. __crook__

ood   7. __stood__

ould 8. __would__   9. __could__
        10. __should__

Pattern Smart

Write the spelling words that have the same pattern as *book*.

11. __shook__   12. __hook__
13. __brook__   14. __crook__

Write the spelling word that has the same pattern as *hood*.

15. __stood__

© Macmillan/McGraw-Hill

| hook | brook | would | should | shook |
| stood | crook | foot | could | soot |

Sentences to Complete

Write a spelling word on each line to complete the sentence.

1. The _____**crook**_____ stole a watch from the shop.

2. An inch is smaller than a _____**foot**_____.

3. Hang your coat up on the _____**hook**_____.

4. We saw ducks swimming in the _____**brook**_____.

5. I _____**stood**_____ up so long my feet hurt.

6. He _____**would**_____ not be able to play in the game.

7. The little boy _____**shook**_____ with fear.

8. Mom knew I _____**could**_____ pick her up at the mall.

9. There was _____**soot**_____ in the fireplace.

10. You _____**should**_____ know the answer to this question.

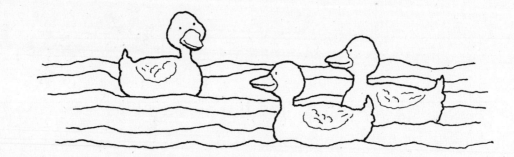

Name_____

**There are six spelling mistakes in the paragraph below.
Circle the misspelled words. Write the words correctly
on the lines below.**

Our class (stud) by the (brouk). It was littered with trash.
We knew we (shood) do something. We got some garbage
bags and gloves. We started picking up the trash. Jan's
(fut) almost slipped into the brook. We had to be careful.
Someone (cuold) get hurt. But we knew everyone (woold) be
very happy that we took care of the brook.

1. _____stood_____ 2. _____brook_____ 3. _____should_____

4. _____foot_____ 5. _____could_____ 6. _____would_____

Writing

**Write about cleaning up something to
make Earth a better place. Use four
spelling words from your list.**

_____

_____

_____

_____

Spelling

Words with Variant
Vowels: *oo, ue,
ui, ew, oe*: Practice

Name_____

Using the Word Study Steps

1. LOOK at the word.

2. SAY the word aloud.

3. STUDY the letters in the word.

4. WRITE the word.

5. CHECK the word.
   Did you spell the word right?
   If not, go back to step 1.

Spelling Words	
root	glue
boot	flew
suit	new
fruit	shoe
clue	canoe

Find and Circle

Circle the ten hidden spelling words.

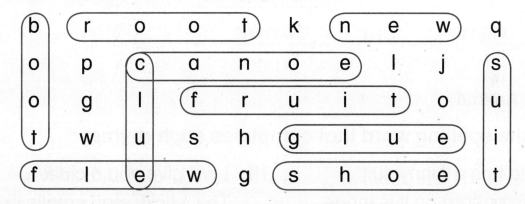

 At Home: Review the Word Study Steps with your child as
you both go over this week's spelling words.

Super Storms • Book 2.2/Unit 4   73

© Macmillan/McGraw-Hill

Spelling

Words with Variant
Vowels: *oo, ue,*
ui, ew, oe: Word Sort

Name_____

| suit | shoe | root | clue | fruit |
| glue | flew | canoe | new | boot |

Word Sort

Look at the spelling words in the box. Write the spelling words that match each spelling pattern.

oo

1. root

2. boot

ue

3. clue

4. glue

ui

5. suit

6. fruit

ew

7. flew

8. new

oe

9. shoe

10. canoe

Rhyme Around

Write the spelling word that completes each rhyme.

11. Dad has a funny suit.
The pattern on it is made
of _____fruit_____.

12. The toy plane flew
because it was
brand _____new_____.

13. We were riding in the canoe
when I lost my right
_____shoe_____.

14. I will give you a clue.
This sticky stuff smells like
_____glue_____.

15. I was digging up the root
when I got mud on my
_____boot_____.

© Macmillan/McGraw-Hill

Name_____

canoe	boot	fruit	glue	new
root	shoe	clue	suit	flew

Match-Ups

Draw a line from each spelling word to its meaning.

1. root — to make stick
2. glue — part of a plant
3. clue — a set of clothes
4. new — a small boat
5. canoe — recently grown or made
6. suit — a hint

Sentences to Complete

Write a spelling word on each line to complete the sentence.

7. My cowboy _____**boot**_____ goes up to my knee.

8. I ate a piece of _____**fruit**_____ for lunch.

9. Which _____**shoe**_____ needs a new lace?

10. Mom _____**flew**_____ to Texas to see her brother.

Spelling

Words with Variant
Vowels: *oo, ue, ui,*
ew, oe: Proofreading

Name _____

There are five spelling mistakes in the paragraph below. Circle the misspelled words. Write the words correctly on the lines below.

Dave had one (buit) on when he saw the weather report. A (nue) cold front was on its way. There was going to be a big winter storm. The big gray clouds were one (clew) that snow would start falling soon. Dave rushed to the airport. Somehow the pilot (floo) the plane and landed it before the storm began. Dave saw his friend get off the plane in a (sute.) Dave gave him a heavy winter coat and gloves for his cold visit to Chicago.

1. ____**boot**____   2. ____**new**____   3. ____**clue**____

4. ____**flew**____   5. ____**suit**____

Writing

Write about a big storm. Use five words from your spelling list.

_____

_____

_____

_____

_____

Name_____

Using the Word Study Steps

1. LOOK at the word.

2. SAY the word aloud.

3. STUDY the letters in the word.

4. WRITE the word.

5. CHECK the word.
   Did you spell the word right?
   If not, go back to step 1.

Spelling Words	
pause	jaw
draw	fawn
launch	hawk
law	raw
fault	crawl

X the Word

Put an X on the word in each row that has a different vowel sound.

1. crawl   la~~mb~~   law

2. w~~ait~~   pause   fault

3. draw   fawn   bo~~nd~~

4. raw   jaw   jo~~in~~

5. lu~~nch~~   launch   hawk

© Macmillan/McGraw-Hill

 At Home: Review the Word Study Steps with your child as you both go over this week's spelling words.

Nutik, the Wolf Pup • **Book 2.2/Unit 4**   **77**

Name_____

| launch | draw | hawk | fawn | pause |
| law | crawl | fault | raw | jaw |

Word Sort

Look at the spelling words in the box. Write the spelling words that have the *au* pattern.

1. launch   2. pause   3. fault

Write the spelling words that have the *aw* pattern.

4. draw   5. hawk   6. fawn

7. law   8. crawl   9. raw

10. jaw

Missing Letter

A letter is missing from each spelling word below. Write the missing letter in the box. Then write the spelling word correctly on the line.

11. pase | u | pause

12. hak | w | hawk

13. lanch | u | launch

14. cral | w | crawl

15. falt | u | fault

© Macmillan/McGraw-Hill

Name_____

| jaw | crawl | fawn | launch | raw |
| pause | draw | law | fault | hawk |

Make a Connection

Write a spelling word to complete each pair of sentences.

1. A child can run. A baby can _____**crawl**_____.

2. A bee is one kind of insect. A _____**hawk**_____ is one kind of bird.

3. I like to paint. You like to _____**draw**_____.

4. A baby cow is called a calf. A baby deer is called a _____**fawn**_____.

5. Our fingers are part of our hand. Our _____**jaw**_____ is part of our mouth.

6. You need to cook the meat. But carrots you can eat _____**raw**_____.

Sentences to Complete

Write a spelling word on each line to complete the sentence.

7. They will _____**launch**_____ the rocket at noon.

8. Is it your _____**fault**_____ that the vase broke?

9. Wearing your seat belt is a _____**law**_____.

10. Stop or _____**pause**_____ after you read the first page.

Name_____

There are five spelling mistakes in the paragraph below. Circle the misspelled words. Write the words correctly on the lines below.

It is very cold and windy in the Arctic. You're likely to see a baby polar bear living there, but not a little (faun.) You might also spot a snowy owl, but not a (hauk.) The Arctic is just too cold for some animals! Animals that have a thick coat of fur can (crauwl,) jump, or play in the snow. You might (pawse) and watch a reindeer or moose make tracks in the snow.

What other Arctic animals can you think of? Try to (drauw) them!

1. ___fawn___   2. ___hawk___   3. ___crawl___
4. ___pause___   5. ___draw___

Writing

Write about one or more animals that can survive in the Arctic. Use five spelling words from your list.

_____

_____

_____

_____

© Macmillan/McGraw-Hill

Name_____

Using the Word Study Steps

1. LOOK at the word.

2. SAY the word aloud.

3. STUDY the letters in the word.

4. WRITE the word.

5. CHECK the word.
   Did you spell the word right?
   If not, go back to step 1.

Spelling Words

clown	round
growl	loud
howl	cloud
brown	house
crown	sound

Puzzle

Solve the puzzle. Circle all the hidden spelling words.

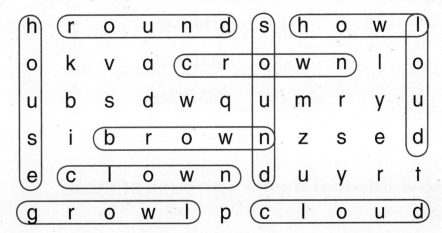

 At Home: Review the Word Study Steps with your child as you both go over this week's spelling words.

Dig, Wait, Listen: A Desert Toad's
Tale • Book 2.2/Unit 5

 81

© Macmillan/McGraw-Hill

Spelling

Words with
Diphthong *ou*: *ow*
and *ou*: Word Sort

Name_____

| clown | round | crown | loud | cloud |
| sound | house | brown | growl | howl |

Word Sort

Look at the spelling words in the box. Fill in the blanks below with spelling words that match each spelling pattern.

ow

1. clown
2. crown
3. brown
4. growl
5. howl

ou

6. round
7. loud
8. cloud
9. sound
10. house

Rhyme Time

Write the spelling words that rhyme with each of these words.

11. pound

round

sound

12. mouse

house

13. owl

growl

howl

Spelling

Words with
Diphthong *ou: ow*
and *ou*: Word Meaning

Name_____

clown	round	crown	loud	cloud
sound	house	brown	growl	howl

Match-Ups

Draw a line from each spelling word to its meaning.

1. clown   shaped like a ball

2. brown   a person who makes you laugh

3. round   a color

4. crown   a building to live in

5. loud   something worn by a king or queen

6. house   noisy

Sentences to Complete

Write a spelling word on the line to complete each sentence.

7. Will the dog _____**growl**_____ at a stranger?

8. The _____**cloud**_____ in the sky was fluffy and white.

9. There was a loud _____**sound**_____ when the alarm went off.

10. I think I heard a coyote _____**howl**_____.

Dig, Wait, Listen: A Desert Toad's
Tale • Book 2.2/Unit 5

Spelling

Words with
Diphthong *ou: ow*
and *ou*: Proofreading

Name_____

**There are six spelling mistakes in the report below.
Circle the misspelled words. Write the words correctly
on the lines below.**

A desert is a hot, dry place. It may look (broun) because
few green plants can survive there. Some animals can
and do live in the desert. You may hear a (lowd)(soond) at
night. What is it? It might be the (houl) of a coyote. Or it
might be the (groowl) of a dingo. Dingoes are like dogs.
Some dangerous animals live in the desert, too. If you see
one of them, go back into your (howse)

1. ___**brown**___	2. ___**loud**___	3. ___**sound**___
4. ___**howl**___	5. ___**growl**___	6. ___**house**___

Writing

**Write a short report about animals that live in the desert.
Use four of the spelling words in your report.**

_____

_____

_____

Spelling

Words with
Diphthong *oi*: *oi*
and *oy*: Practice

Name_____

Using the Word Study Steps

1. LOOK at the word.

2. SAY the word aloud.

3. STUDY the letters in the word.

4. WRITE the word.

5. CHECK the word.
   Did you spell the word right?
   If not, go back to step 1.

Spelling Words	
soil	oil
broil	toy
moist	joy
point	soy
boil	royal

X the Word

Find two words in each row with the same vowel sound and spelling pattern. Cross out the other word that does not belong.

1. royal   cr~~a~~wl   soy

2. soil   moist   m~~o~~st

3. br~~o~~wn   broil   oil

4. joy   j~~ob~~   toy

5. boil   point   po~~i~~nt

At Home: Review the Word Study Steps with your child as you both go over this week's spelling words.

© Macmillan/McGraw-Hill

Name_____

boil	moist	joy	toy	point
broil	soil	soy	royal	oil

Word Sort

Look at the spelling words in the box. Write the spelling words that have the *oi* pattern.

1. _____boil_____   2. _____moist_____   3. _____broil_____

4. _____soil_____   5. _____oil_____   6. _____point_____

Write the spelling words that have the *oy* pattern.

7. _____joy_____   8. _____toy_____   9. _____soy_____

10. _____royal_____

Missing Letter

A letter is missing from each spelling word below. Write the missing letter in the box. Then write the spelling word correctly on the line.

11. brol [i] _____broil_____

12. roal [y] _____royal_____

13. moit [s] _____moist_____

14. pont [i] _____point_____

15. sil [o] _____soil_____

Spelling

Words with
Diphthong *oi*: *oi*
and *oy*: Word Meaning

Name_____

| boil | moist | joy | toy | point |
| broil | soil | soy | royal | oil |

Sentences to Complete

Write a spelling word on each line to complete the sentence.

1. Mom fried the fish in _____**oil**_____ .

2. The new baby brought much _____**joy**_____ to her family.

3. I can _____**broil**_____ the meat in the oven.

4. Water made the towel feel _____**moist**_____ .

5. The _____**royal**_____ family sat on their thrones.

Definitions

Write the spelling word for each definition.

6. An object that children play with _____**toy**_____

7. A small mark or dot used in writing _____**point**_____

8. Dirt that plants grow in _____**soil**_____

9. To heat water until it bubbles _____**boil**_____

10. A sauce used on foods _____**soy**_____

Spelling

Words with
Diphthong *oi*: *oi*
and *oy*: Proofreading

Name_____

There are six spelling mistakes in the paragraph below. Circle the misspelled words. Write the words correctly on the lines below.

Once I was in a play about a king and queen. The stage was a ⟨rouyal⟩ castle. The queen did not cook. She had her servant ⟨boel⟩ water for her tea. The king was very funny. He put ⟨soey⟩ sauce on everything he ate! I played the king and queen's child. I brought them great ⟨joiy⟩ My favorite ⟨toiy⟩ in the castle was a nutcracker. The nutcracker squeaked when I used it. I learned how to ⟨oel⟩ it so it did not make any noise. The play was fun to be in!

1. **royal**   2. **boil**   3. **soy**

4. **joy**   5. **toy**   6. **oil**

Writing

Write about acting in a play. Use four or five of your spelling words. Circle the spelling words you use.

_____

_____

_____

_____

© Macmillan/McGraw-Hill

Name_____

Using the Word Study Steps

1. LOOK at the word.

2. SAY the word aloud.

3. STUDY the letters in the word.

4. WRITE the word.

5. CHECK the word.
   Did you spell the word right?
   If not, go back to step 1.

<table>
<tr><td colspan="2">Spelling Words</td></tr>
<tr><td>alone</td><td>agree</td></tr>
<tr><td>ago</td><td>above</td></tr>
<tr><td>again</td><td>awake</td></tr>
<tr><td>away</td><td>idea</td></tr>
<tr><td>alike</td><td>comma</td></tr>
</table>

Find and Circle

Circle the ten hidden spelling words in the puzzle.

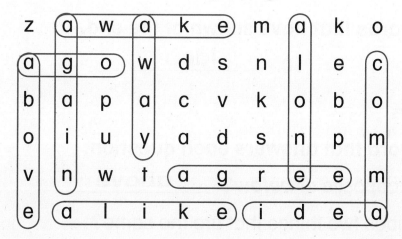

At Home: Review the Word Study Steps with your child as
you both go over this week's spelling words.

Name_____

alone	comma	alike	awake	idea
ago	again	away	agree	above

Word Sort

Look at the spelling words in the box. Write the spelling words that have schwa at the beginning.

1. alone

2. alike

3. awake

4. ago

5. again

6. away

7. agree

8. above

Write the spelling words that have schwa at the end.

9. comma

10. idea

Questions and Answers

Write the spelling word that answers each question.

11. What word is the opposite of **below**? above

12. What word describes two things that are the same?

alike

13. What word is a punctuation mark? comma

14. What word means "to have a thought"? idea

15. What word means "you have the same opinion"? agree

Name _____

| alone | comma | alike | awake | idea |
| ago | again | away | agree | above |

Sentences to Complete

Write a spelling word on each line to complete the sentence.

1. The twins dress __alike__ every day.

2. We played the game over and over __again__.

3. There is a __comma__ in the last sentence.

4. I __agree__ with your decision to stay home.

5. The shelf is up __above__ the table.

6. Are you __awake__ or sleeping?

7. Whose __idea__ was it to clean up the basement?

8. Sam moved far __away__ last year.

9. When you are by yourself, you are __alone__.

10. Long __ago__ people did not have cars to drive.

Name_____

**There are six spelling mistakes in the paragraph below.
Circle the misspelled words. Write the words correctly
on the lines below.**

Long (aego) there was an explorer named Christopher
Columbus. Columbus had the (ideea) that he would
discover new lands. Columbus sailed (eway) on several
voyages. He did not sail (ulone). He had a crew on each
of his ships. None of his trips was exactly (elike). He did
not travel to the same place over and over (aigain). He
discovered many new places in the Caribbean and South
America.

1. ___ago___ 2. ___idea___ 3. ___away___
4. ___alone___ 5. ___alike___ 6. ___again___

Writing

**Write about an explorer who came to America.
Use four words from your spelling list.**

_____

_____

_____

Name_____

Using the Word Study Steps

1. LOOK at the word.

2. SAY the word aloud.

3. STUDY the letters in the word.

4. WRITE the word.

5. CHECK the word.
   Did you spell the word right?
   If not, go back to step 1.

Spelling Words

knee	wrist
knife	wren
knot	thumb
gnaw	lamb
sign	debt

X the Word

Look at the spelling words in each row. Find two words in each row with the same silent letter. Cross out the other word that does not belong.

1. lamb   thumb   wr~~e~~n

2. knee   wr~~i~~st   knot

3. gnaw   sign   la~~m~~b

4. wr~~e~~n   debt   thumb

5. s~~i~~gn   knife   knee

 At Home: Review the Word Study Steps with your child as you both go over this week's spelling words.

The Ugly Vegetables

93

Book 2.2/Unit 5

© Macmillan/McGraw-Hill

Name_____

wrist	gnaw	debt	knife	thumb
knee	sign	wren	lamb	knot

Word Sort

Look at the spelling words in the box. Match each word to a spelling pattern. Write the spelling words on the lines below.

Silent *w*

1. wrist
2. wren

Silent *g*

6. gnaw
7. sign

Silent *k*

3. knife
4. knee
5. knot

Silent *b*

8. debt
9. thumb
10. lamb

Missing Letter

The silent letter is missing from each spelling word below. Write the missing letter in the box. Then write the spelling word correctly on the line.

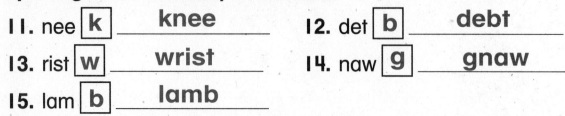

11. nee k̲ knee
12. det b̲ debt
13. rist w̲ wrist
14. naw g̲ gnaw
15. lam b̲ lamb

© Macmillan/McGraw-Hill

Name_____

| wren | knot | lamb | knee | debt |
| knife | gnaw | wrist | thumb | sign |

Match-Ups

Draw a line from each spelling word to its meaning.

1. lamb   a part of the arm

2. wrist   a baby sheep

3. knife   a part of the leg

4. knee   a bird

5. wren   a cutting blade

Sentences to Complete

Write a spelling word on each line to complete the sentence.

6. Your shoelace has a big _____**knot**_____.

7. The _____**sign**_____ on the door tells visitors where to go.

8. Your _____**thumb**_____ is one of your five fingers.

9. If you owe money, you are in _____**debt**_____.

10. The beaver will _____**gnaw**_____ on the tree bark.

Name_____

There are five spelling mistakes in the paragraph below. Circle the misspelled words. Write the words correctly on the lines below.

Grandpa and I planted a garden. Grandpa's (rist) hurt, so I dug the holes and dropped in the seeds. I had one (nee) on the ground as I covered the seeds with dirt. Then we made a (signe) for each vegetable we planted. Grandpa says that I have a green (thum.) When we finished, we saw a (ren) flying by. Now Grandpa and I are going to make a scarecrow to keep the birds away!

1. ____wrist____   2. ____knee____   3. ____sign____

4. ____thumb____   5. ____wren____

Writing

Write about planting and taking care of a garden. Use five spelling words. Circle the spelling words you use.

_____

_____

_____

Name_____

Using the Word Study Steps

1. LOOK at the word.

2. SAY the word aloud.

3. STUDY the letters
   in the word.

4. WRITE the word.

5. CHECK the word.
   Did you spell the word right?
   If not, go back to step 1.

Find and Circle

Where are the spelling words?

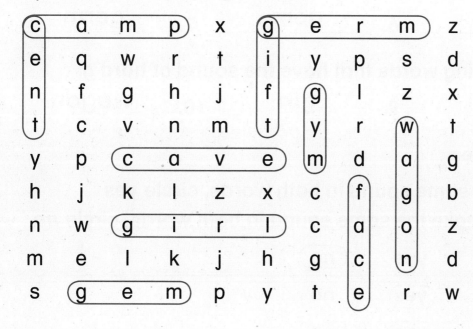

```
c  a  m  p  x   g  e  r  m  z
e  q  w  r  t   i  y  p  s  d
n  f  g  h  j   f  g  l  z  x
t  c  v  n  m   t  y  r  w  t
y  p  c  a  v  e  m  d  a  g
h  j  k  l  z  x  c  f  g  b
n  w  g  i  r  l  c  a  o  z
m  e  l  k  j  h  g  c  n  d
s  g  e  m  p  y  t  e  r  w
```

At Home: Review the Word Study Steps with your child as
you both go over this week's spelling words.

© Macmillan/McGraw-Hill

Name_____

| cave | cent | gift | gym | face |
| camp | girl | gem | wagon | germ |

Word Sort

Look at the spelling words in the box. Write the spelling
words that have the sound of soft *c*.

1. ___cent___   2. ___face___

Write the spelling words that have the sound of hard *c*.

3. ___cave___   4. ___camp___

Write the spelling words that have the sound of soft *g*.

5. ___gym___   6. ___gem___   7. ___germ___

Write the spelling words that have the sound of hard *g*.

8. ___gift___   9. ___girl___   10. ___wagon___

Sounds the Same

If *c* makes the same sound in both words, circle *yes*.
If *c* does not make the same sound in both words, circle *no*.

11. cave, face   yes   (no)

12. camp, cave   (yes)   no

13. face, cent   (yes)   no

Name _____

wagon	gift	camp	cent	gym
face	germ	cave	girl	gem

Match-Ups

Draw a line from each spelling word to its meaning.

1. wagon   the front of the head

2. gift   a cart used by children

3. face   a place where there are tents

4. gym   a present

5. camp   a precious stone

6. gem   a room for games and sports

Sentences to Complete

Write a spelling word on each line to complete the sentence.

7. Bats were flying inside the dark _____**cave**_____.

8. One _____**cent**_____ is the same as one penny.

9. Sandy is the name of a _____**girl**_____ in my class.

10. The _____**germ**_____ made the little boy sick.

Name_____

There are five spelling mistakes in the paragraph below. Circle the misspelled words. Write the words correctly on the lines below.

At (kamp) we learned a lot about the sun and the moon. Why is it dark inside a (kave)? It is dark because there is no sunlight. The sun is like a (jem) that brightly shines during the day. At night, it is the moon that shines on your (fase) The moon and stars light up the night sky. Sometimes the moon looks round like a one (scent) coin. Other times you can only see a sliver of the moon. Look up in the sky now. What do you see?

1. _____camp_____   2. _____cave_____   3. _____gem_____

4. _____face_____   5. _____cent_____

Writing

Write about the day sky and the night sky. Use five spelling words from your list.

_____

_____

_____

_____

Name_____

Using the Word Study Steps

1. LOOK at the word.

2. SAY the word aloud.

3. STUDY the letters in the word.

4. WRITE the word.

5. CHECK the word.
   Did you spell the word right?
   If not, go back to step 1.

Spelling Words	
cage	barge
page	bulge
judge	change
lodge	range
large	hinge

Puzzle

Solve the puzzle. Circle the hidden spelling words.

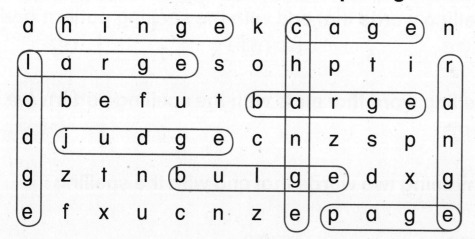

```
a  h  i  n  g  e  k  c  a  g  e  n
l  a  r  g  e  s  o  h  p  t  i  r
o  b  e  f  u  t  b  a  r  g  e  a
d  j  u  d  g  e  c  n  z  s  p  n
g  z  t  n  b  u  l  g  e  d  x  g
e  f  x  u  c  n  z  e  p  a  g  e
```

 At Home: Review the Word Study Steps with your child as you both go over this week's spelling words.

Name_____

| large | bulge | range | cage | lodge |
| page | change | judge | hinge | barge |

Word Sort

Look at the spelling words in the box. Write the spelling words that end with the spelling pattern *dge*.

1. lodge
2. judge

Write the spelling words that end with the spelling pattern *rge*.

3. large
4. barge

Write the spelling words that end with the spelling pattern *nge*.

5. range
6. change
7. hinge

Write the spelling word that ends with the spelling pattern *lge*.

8. bulge

Write the remaining two words that end with the spelling pattern *ge*.

9. cage
10. page

Rhyme Time

Write the spelling words that rhyme with each of these words.

rage 11. cage 12. page

strange 13. range 14. change

budge 15. judge

Name_____

large	bulge	range	cage	lodge
page	change	judge	hinge	barge

Sentences to Complete

Write a spelling word on each line to complete the sentence.

1. Jose's pet rabbit lives in a __**cage**__.

2. The __**hinge**__ on the door needs to be oiled.

3. Turn to the last __**page**__ of your book.

4. Do you think Sam will __**change**__ his mind?

5. The __**large**__ box did not fit in the closet.

6. The __**judge**__ banged her gavel in court.

7. People live in the ski __**lodge**__ all winter.

8. Your stomach might __**bulge**__ if you eat too much.

9. The __**barge**__ floated down the river.

10. The age __**range**__ is between six and ten years.

© Macmillan/McGraw-Hill

Spelling

Words with *ge*, *dge*,
rge, *lge*, *nge*:
Proofreading

Name_____

**There are five spelling mistakes in the paragraph below.
Circle the misspelled words. Write the words correctly
on the lines below.**

Last Sunday we had a surprise party for Grandma's
birthday. The party was at Grandpa's (lodje) in a (largge)
room. We had to (chanje) how the tables were arranged
so everyone had a place to sit. The time (rangge) for the
party was from four o'clock to eight o'clock, but everyone
came early to yell "Surprise!" Grandma was so happy to
see her friends. Even the (juge) who lives next door came.
Grandma can't wait until her next birthday!

1. ___lodge___   2. ___large___   3. ___change___

4. ___range___   5. ___judge___

Writing

**Write about a special family celebration. Use five words
from the spelling list.**

_____

_____

_____

_____

Name_____

Using the Word Study Steps

1. LOOK at the word.

2. SAY the word aloud.

3. STUDY the letters in the word.

4. WRITE the word.

5. CHECK the word.
   Did you spell the word right?
   If not, go back to step 1.

Spelling Words	
star	dare
shark	hair
care	pair
stare	chair
rare	fair

X the Word

Find two words in each row with the same vowel sound and spelling pattern. Cross out the other word that does not belong.

1. pair   chair   ch~~a~~rm

2. star   st~~o~~mp   shark

3. c~~o~~rd   care   rare

4. dare   st~~o~~rm   stare

5. hair   fair   f~~o~~rm

At Home: Review the Word Study Steps with your child as you both go over this week's spelling words.

Spelling

Words with *r*-Controlled
Vowels: *ar, are, air*:
Word Sort

Name_____

fair	care	star	hair	pair
shark	stare	dare	rare	chair

Word Sort

Look at the spelling words in the box. Match each word
with a spelling pattern.

ar   1. ___star___   2. ___shark___

are   3. ___care___   4. ___stare___

5. ___dare___   6. ___rare___

air   7. ___fair___   8. ___hair___

9. ___pair___   10. ___chair___

Misfit Letter

An extra letter has been added to each spelling word
below. Draw a line through the letter that does not
belong. Write the word correctly on the line.

11. ca/ire ___care___   12. fair/e ___fair___

13. pair/e ___pair___   14. sha/irk ___shark___

15. chai/er ___chair___

Spelling

Words with *r*-Controlled
Vowels: *ar*, *are*, *air*:
Word Meaning

Name _____

fair	care	star	hair	pair
shark	stare	dare	rare	chair

Definitions

Write the spelling word for each definition.

1. A piece of furniture that you sit on   **chair**

2. Not common   **rare**

3. A large fish   **shark**

4. An object seen in the night sky   **star**

5. To look at something with eyes open wide   **stare**

6. Two similar things used together   **pair**

7. A festival or carnival   **fair**

Sentences to Complete

Write a spelling word on each line to complete the sentence.

8. Wash your _____**hair**_____ in the shower.

9. I _____**dare**_____ you to go to school dressed like a monkey.

10. Pat takes _____**care**_____ of her new puppy.

Spelling

Words with *r*-Controlled
Vowels: *ar, are, air*:
Proofreading

Name_____

**There are six spelling mistakes in the paragraph below.
Circle the misspelled words. Write the words correctly
on the lines below.**

   Everyone in our class is writing a book. Mark's book is
about a (shairk.) Jeff's book is about a shooting (starr.) My
book is about how to take (cair) of your (haire.) After we
write our books, we will illustrate them. Then we will sit
in an author's (chare) and read our stories to each other.
We might also have a book (faire) so the entire school can
read our books.

1. _____shark_____   2. _____star_____   3. _____care_____

4. _____hair_____   5. _____chair_____   6. _____fair_____

Writing

**Be an author! Write a
story about something
you know about or enjoy
doing. Use four words from your spelling list.**

_____

_____

_____

_____

© Macmillan/McGraw-Hill

Spelling

Words with *r*-Controlled
Vowels: *er, eer, ere, ear*:
Practice

Name_____

Using the Word Study Steps

1. LOOK at the word.

2. SAY the word aloud.

3. STUDY the letters in the word.

4. WRITE the word.

5. CHECK the word.
   Did you spell the word right?
   If not, go back to step 1.

Spelling Words	
near	queer
dear	verb
ear	perch
deer	here
steer	where

Find and Circle

Where are the spelling words?

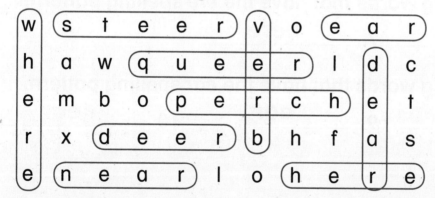

 At Home: Review the Word Study Steps with your child as you both go over this week's spelling words.

Music of the Stone Age 109
Book 2.2/Unit 6

Name_____

near	where	deer	verb	perch
ear	steer	here	dear	queer

Word Sort

Look at the spelling words in the box. Write the spelling words that have the *er* spelling pattern.

1. _____verb_____   2. _____perch_____

Write the spelling words that have the *eer* spelling pattern.

3. _____deer_____   4. _____steer_____   5. _____queer_____

Write the spelling words that have the *ere* spelling pattern.

6. _____where_____   7. _____here_____

Write the spelling words that have the *ear* spelling pattern.

8. _____near_____   9. _____ear_____   10. _____dear_____

Find the Pattern

Read each group of words. Circle the word that does not fit the pattern.

11. near, ear, (deer)

12. here, (verb,) where

13. (perch,) steer, queer

14. (where) dear, near

15. (deer,) perch, verb

Spelling

Words with *r*-Controlled
Vowels: *er, eer, ere, ear*:
Word Meanings

Name_____

near	where	deer	verb	perch
ear	steer	here	dear	queer

Match-Ups

Draw a line from each spelling word to its meaning.

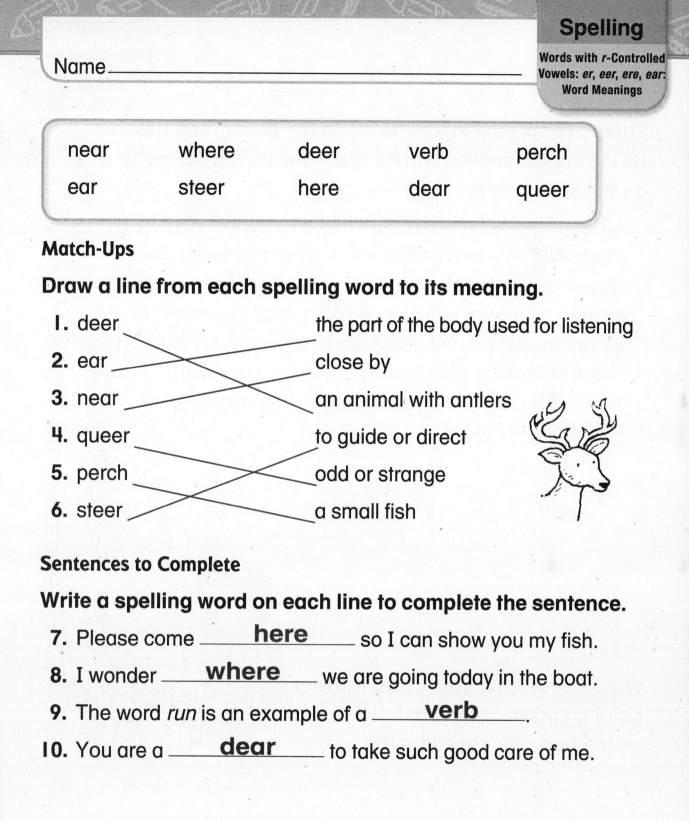

1. deer   the part of the body used for listening

2. ear   close by

3. near   an animal with antlers

4. queer   to guide or direct

5. perch   odd or strange

6. steer   a small fish

Sentences to Complete

Write a spelling word on each line to complete the sentence.

7. Please come _____**here**_____ so I can show you my fish.

8. I wonder _____**where**_____ we are going today in the boat.

9. The word *run* is an example of a _____**verb**_____.

10. You are a _____**dear**_____ to take such good care of me.

Name_____

There are six spelling mistakes in the paragraph below. Circle the misspelled words. Write the words correctly on the lines below.

My mom is an artist. She has a studio (wheer) she works every day. We live (nere) the woods so my mom draws lots of animals. One day she drew a (der) that she saw right outside her window. A fisherman lives next door, so my mom painted a picture of a (peerch) for him. My mom painted a picture of a cool race car for me. I have it hanging (heer) in my bedroom. I love that picture. It is very (deere) to me.

1. **where** 2. **near** 3. **deer**

4. **perch** 5. **here** 6. **dear**

Writing

Write about what you would draw or paint if you were an artist. Use four words from your spelling list.

_____

_____

_____

Spelling

Words with *r*-Controlled
Vowels: *or, ore, oar*:
Practice

Name_____

Using the Word Study Steps

1. LOOK at the word.

2. SAY the word aloud.

3. STUDY the letters
   in the word.

4. WRITE the word.

5. CHECK the word.
   Did you spell the word right?
   If not, go back to step 1.

Spelling Words	
more	roar
tore	board
wore	port
store	north
oar	fort

Find and Circle

Where are the spelling words?

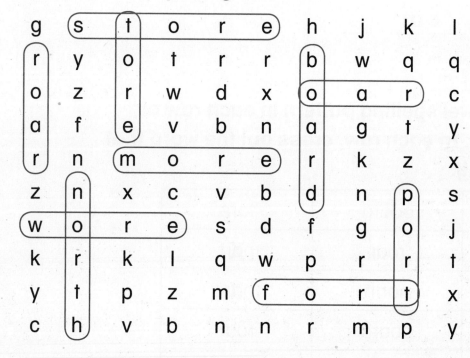

 At Home: Review the Word Study Steps with your child as
you both go over this week's spelling words.

Spelling

Words with *r*-Controlled
Vowels: *or, ore, oar:*
Word Sort

Name_____

north	port	store	roar	board
oar	more	wore	tore	fort

Look at the spelling words in the box. Match each word with a spelling pattern.

or

1. _____north_____   2. _____port_____

3. _____fort_____

ore

4. _____store_____   5. _____more_____

6. _____wore_____   7. _____tore_____

oar

8. _____roar_____   9. _____board_____

10. _____oar_____

X the Word

Look at the vowel spelling pattern in each row of spelling words. In each row, cross out the word that does not belong.

store	bo~~a~~rd	tore
oar	roar	p~~o~~rt
fort	north	m~~o~~re
w~~o~~re	board	roar
north	port	st~~o~~re

African-American Inventors
Book 2.2/Unit 6

© Macmillan/McGraw-Hill

Name_____

north	port	store	roar	board
oar	more	wore	tore	fort

Definitions

Write the spelling word for each definition.

1. Past tense of *tear* _____**tore**_____

2. A paddle used to row a boat _____**oar**_____

3. A loud rumbling sound _____**roar**_____

4. A harbor _____**port**_____

5. The direction opposite of south _____**north**_____

6. A place where things are sold _____**store**_____

7. An army post _____**fort**_____

Sentences to Complete

Write a spelling word on each line to complete the sentence.

8. I need _____**more**_____ glue to finish my art project.

9. Sue _____**wore**_____ her red dress to the party.

10. The wooden _____**board**_____ had nails pounded into it.

© Macmillan/McGraw-Hill

Name_____

Spelling

Words with *r*-Controlled
Vowels: *or, ore, oar*:
Proofreading

There are six spelling mistakes in the paragraph below. Circle the misspelled words. Write the words correctly on the lines below.

Inventors have dreamed up many new things over the years. There are (moar) inventions today than ever before. Someone invented an (oare) to row a boat. Someone else invented a (bord) game called checkers. Long ago, if you (woore) your jeans and (toare) them, you would need to mend them by hand. Today you can fix them on a sewing machine. Or you can drive to a big department (stoore) and buy a new pair. What other inventions can you think of?

1. ___more___   2. ___oar___

3. ___board___   4. ___wore___

5. ___tore___   6. ___store___

Writing

Write about your own idea for an invention. Use four words from the spelling list.

_____

_____

_____

Spelling

Words with *r*-Controlled
Vowels: *ire, ier, ure*:
Practice

Name_____

Using the Word Study Steps

1. LOOK at the word.

2. SAY the word aloud.

3. STUDY the letters in the word.

4. WRITE the word.

5. CHECK the word.
   Did you spell the word right?
   If not, go back to step 1.

Spelling Words

fire	flier
wire	crier
hire	sure
tire	cure
drier	pure

Puzzle

Solve the puzzle. Circle all of the hidden spelling words.

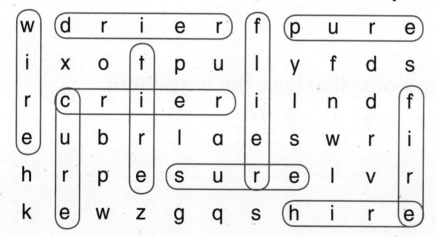

At Home: Review the Word Study Steps with your child as
you both go over this week's spelling words.

Babu's Song • **Book 2.2/Unit 6**　117

Spelling

Words with *r*-Controlled
Vowels: *ire*, *ier*, *ure*:
Word Sort

Name_____

wire	sure	pure	crier	fire
flier	cure	tire	hire	drier

Word Sort

Look at the spelling words in the box. Write the spelling words that have the *ire* pattern.

1. ____wire____   2. ____fire____

3. ____tire____   4. ____hire____

Write the spelling words that have the *ier* pattern.

5. ____crier____   6. ____flier____

7. ____drier____

Write the spelling words that have the *ure* pattern.

8. ____sure____   9. ____pure____

10. ____cure____

Match Patterns

If the spelling words in each row have the same pattern, circle *yes*. If they do not have the same pattern, circle *no*.

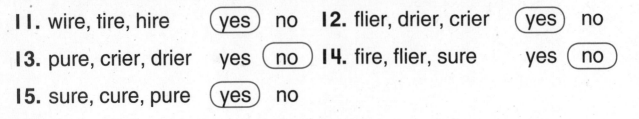

11. wire, tire, hire   (yes)   no   12. flier, drier, crier   (yes)   no

13. pure, crier, drier   yes   (no)   14. fire, flier, sure   yes   (no)

15. sure, cure, pure   (yes)   no

Name

Spelling
Words with *r*-Controlled
Vowels: *ire*, *ier*, *ure*:
Word Meaning

| wire | sure | pure | crier | fire |
| flier | cure | tire | hire | drier |

Match-Ups

Draw a line from each spelling word to its meaning.

1. crier   not dirty or polluted; clean

2. pure   a thin rod of metal

3. wire   a person who cries

4. flier   to make well

5. cure   a person or thing that flies

Sentences to Complete

Write a spelling word on each line to complete the sentence.

6. Will you __**hire**__ me to do the job?

7. The car has a flat __**tire**__ that needs to be changed.

8. Are you __**sure**__ you want to play outside in the rain?

9. My wet towel felt __**drier**__ after it was in the sun.

10. We used logs to make a __**fire**__ at camp.

Spelling

Words with *r*-Controlled
Vowels: *ire, ier, ure*:
Proofreading

Name _____

**There are six spelling mistakes in the paragraph below.
Circle the misspelled words. Write the words correctly
on the lines below.**

I am flying to visit my grandpa who lives in Italy. The
plane should be taking off right now, but it has a flat
(tiere.) I (shure) hope it gets fixed soon! Now the tire is fixed,
but there is a loose (wier.) This needs to be fixed too. At
last, this (fliere) is ready to take off! I know it can fly in this
rainstorm. I think it will be (driere) when the plane lands
in Rome. I hope there is (puir) sunshine so my grandpa
and I can go sightseeing!

I. _____tire_____ 2. _____sure_____ 3. _____wire_____

4. _____flier_____ 5. _____drier_____ 6. _____pure_____

Writing

**Write about visiting a relative who
lives far away. Use four words from
your spelling list.**

_____

_____

_____

_____